LOVE AND OTHER COLLISIONS

LVE

AND OTHER COLLISIONS

Poems

Joseph Mills

Press 53
Winston-Salem, NC

Press 53
PO Box 30314
Winston-Salem, NC 27130

First Edition

Cover design by Kevin Watson

Author photo by Danielle Tarmey

Printed on acid-free paper

ISBN 978-0-9825760-8-3

For my family

CONTENTS

WHERE WE ARE NOW

LEARNING TO FALL

ACKNOWLEDGMENTS

Thanks to the following publications where these poems (or earlier versions) first appeared:

Apparatus: "Among Schoolchildren"
Blue Fifth: "The Fist as a Unit of Measurement"
Foliate Oak: "The Bruiser," "Edges," "The Guardian," "Neighbors"
Foundling Review: "Alignment," "Singing to the Woman Who Used to Be My Mother"
Ghoti Magazine: "A Midnight Call About the End of the World," "Beacon," "Love Me Do"
The Innisfree Poetry Journal: "Accidents," "Drivers"
MountainRise: "Casting," "Cutters," "Dispersal," "Learning to Fall"
Parent: Wise Magazine: "Baking with My Daughter"
Quicksilver: "Commencement," "The Watch"
Review Americana: "A Road Labeled 'F-E-A-R'," (published as "Fear")
Rattle: "Conversation"
The Tower: "Losing Paris," "Objects in Motion," "Shaking Hands," "Waiters"
To The Bone: "Education"
Umbrella: "Left Behind," "On Looking at Frida Kahlo's Little Deer"
Utah English Journal: "Spelling Lessons"

I also am indebted to Sean O'Grady, and the MakeGroup of Bob King, Betsy Towns, and Dean Wilcox.

COMMENCEMENT

The Bruiser

By the time my dad took me
to see him at the Coliseum,
he was old, with puckered skin,
a sagging belly, arm webbing,
but still growling and threatening
the way he had for decades.

He never wore a mask, cape,
or costume, but he had a patch
on his forehead that was filled
with cow's blood. When he got
hit, red liquid would spurt out,
sending the crowd into a frenzy.

We all knew about the patch
and appreciated it, recognizing
it was a guarantee that those
who had gathered would have
a blood offering even when
his own body didn't break open.

The scars covering his flesh,
the bumps of badly set bones,
the mutilated body a testament,
not to the pain he could inflict,
but to what he could take and keep
going, this is why fathers

brought their sons to see and cheer
the cigar-chewing, ugly, old man,
The Bruiser, the one who showed
how you could make something
of your life if only you could stand
enough punishment over the years.

Spelling Lessons

The hardest words to spell weren't the longest,
but the tricksters, the ones like "subtle" trying
to smuggle its "b" past you or "government"
with its "r" and "m" folding over that first "n"
and making it shut up. To help with these,
Mrs. Nelson would emphasize some oddity,
like a naturalist explaining an animal's markings
or eating habits. She showed us how "weird"
refuses to conform to the saying "i before e
except after c," making the word itself weird;
she loved to say, *"when –ing comes to stay
little e runs away,"* and that to spell "separate"
we only had to remember it had "a rat" inside.
This helped us with tests and spelling bees,
but it also made me uneasy to be so aware
of the insides of words, to recognize the effort
it must take the "e" in "strength" to hold those
seven consonants together. And where did all
those little e's run away to? Did they find refuge
on eye charts, in comic book effects, as typoes?
And that rat? How did it get there? If it was dead,
that was weird, but worse was to think of it alive,
trapped inside, trying to gnaw out. You no longer
could use words casually when you recognized some
were cages whose parts might suddenly separate,
freeing an animal onto a page or into your mouth.

Neighbors

We would take turns asking him
about the government, crime rates,
gasoline and food prices, just to hear
those expletives, the damning to hells,
the putting of people in places
and positions we couldn't imagine
on our own. Once he got going,
he would slam his hands against
his wheelchair hard enough to shake
the porch, and when he slowed down
all you had to say was "Really?"
to get another five minutes or more.

If he would have had a coin slot,
we gladly would have dropped in
our allowance for the chance to hear
those full-throated arias, those seemingly
infinite variations of contempt and rage
at how callous human beings could be.

Child's Play

In the winter, our favorite playground game
was "Murder the Bum," which, when the nuns
weren't listening, we called, "Smear the Queer."
You threw a ball in the air, then tackled the one
who caught it. There was no way to win. At best
someone might manage to run longer than normal
and avoid getting a black eye or bloody nose,
but eventually a person was always cornered.
The game taught us this and the full-throated joy
of the chase, the righteous feeling that anyone
with the ball deserved to be taken down, smeared,
and yet we all wanted to be the bum, the queer,
the outsider to be punished. Were we showing
we could take it? That fundamental lesson
of Good Friday? Did we hope for a moment
of grace, a day when we might run, uncaught,
until the bell rang? Decades later, a snowfall
still makes me shiver as I imagine reaching out
for the ball, tucking it close, and trying to break
from the pack across that unbroken whiteness,
the desperate pleasure of running, the laughter
as I am cornered, pulled down and murdered.

Left Behind

After Sunday dinner, my brother and sister
washed the dishes while I would be handed
the platter to take to the basement. There
I'd screw the meat grinder to the worktable,
stuff wedges of pot roast into its gray funnel,
and turn the wooden handle so dark ribbons
spiraled into white Tupperware. Above me
I would hear footsteps, the usual arguing,
sometimes laughter, sometimes singing,
but by the time I finished and ascended,
the kitchen would be clean and empty.
I would put the bowl in the fridge,
dismantle the grinder, and wash the grease
from its gears. Now, seeing bumper stickers
warning, "In case of Rapture this car
will not have a driver," I wonder if I know
already how that will feel. Maybe it will
be like coming up the stairs to find only
the stove light on, the dishwasher humming,
everyone you know gone, and your hands
full of slick metal and leftover meat.

The Rending Intimacies of Collisions

When Kevin snuck out his Mom's Nova
to come show me his new driver's license,
I didn't realize he had brought Bingo
until I opened the door, and the dog ran
straight into the street where she was hit
by a Buick station wagon. She was dead
before we got to her, and Kevin sprinted
back to the Chevy and peeled out, swerving
past the body. The woman who hit Bingo
couldn't stop crying, saying she had been
trying a different way home from the grocery.
Eventually she gave me a red plaid blanket
from the back seat, one she kept "for picnics,"
and I wrapped the dog up like a delicate gift.

I waited a week for Kevin to call or come over,
but he didn't, so finally I stopped by his locker,
held out the collar, and asked if he wanted it,
maybe to give his mother since Bingo was hers.
He looked at me as if he couldn't believe
what an asshole I was being. As he shoved
past, I felt a combination of embarrassment,
nausea, and exhilaration just like that time
Tony had shown me a magazine he stole
from his Dad's closet and explained the photos
were of people fucking, which was banging
into each other really hard. When I asked,
"Why?" he shrugged as if it was just something
grown-ups did and someday we would do it too.

Before Cable TV When People Used to Amuse Themselves the Old Fashioned Way

Hanging out in the garage one night
we came up with the idea of filling
buckets with samplings from the cans
surrounding us, the paint thinners,
kerosene, gasoline, charcoal lighters,
anything with a "flammable" label.
Tony kept insisting we could use
ones with an "inflammable" warning
as well, but that didn't make sense
so we mocked him until he shut up.

We carried the buckets up the hill
and spread them on Mickey's lot,
the one where the summer before
a couple had parked a van one night.
Bobby said he heard our dads laughing
about how "that crazy son-of-a-bitch
Mickey" had snuck up and waited until
their clothes were off before he broke
out the headlights with a shotgun
and pointed it in the driver's window.
We flicked matches, one at a time,
onto the stain, but nothing happened.
Finally, disillusioned and reeking
of petroleum, we returned to the garage
where we heard the "whoompf" and
shards of light started ricocheting off
buildings. We sprinted up to the fire

and smothered it with trash cans, smiling
all the while, our young crackling faces
iridescent from the joy of our burning.

Education

My junior year in high school I worked
forty hours a week at a restaurant
where I learned how to cut a crate
of lettuce in under fifteen minutes,
how to make fifty pounds of dough,
how people act differently when they
become Assistant Manager. Listening
to the waitresses, who were married,
separated, divorced, older than me
by five to forty years, I learned how
the world was rather than how
I had been led to believe it would be.
No matter what they talked about—
rent, children, hair, bad boyfriends,
the value of community college courses,
whether to make the manager a cake
shaped like a penis for his birthday
or if those should only be for staff—
Trish, the head waitress, would say,
"It's always the same old, same old,
isn't it, girls? Hard work and humping.
That's what it always comes down to."
One Saturday night, when I insisted
a waitress with two kids should stop
smoking and threw her Marlboros
in a sink of water, I learned what it meant
to be cussed out by someone who knew
what she was doing, and I was shocked,
not by the ferocity, but the realization

I deserved it. On my break, I ran over
to Kroger's for a new carton. I apologized,
explaining how my dad smoked a pack
a day, and I thought he would probably die
of cancer. She started crying, hugged me,
switched breaks to smoke a quick one,
and later, after closing, in the parking lot,
taught me how powerful an apology could be.

Objects in Motion

Our science teacher was a retiree
from GM. We suspected the school
got him cheap because he was senile.
To demonstrate some law of physics,
he led the class to the parking lot,
started his car, put it in gear,
and let it slam into the building.
"You see," he said. We nodded,
although we didn't. To explain
momentum, he described how
they would put pretty secretaries
on the paint shaker; after it stopped,
"some parts of them kept moving."
When Cathy Antonioni asked how
prettiness was factored in the equation,
he looked at her, puzzled. He liked
to say, "Given enough time,
water will dissolve a battleship."
We would nod at that too,
then, finally, we were cut loose
from his ramblings and from all
the other equally crazy old teachers.
We moved away from each another,
steaming confidently into our lives,
as sleek and hard as the steel
our fathers molded at the factory,
not yet aware how the years
would reveal at least some
of what he said was true:
we were the battleships,
and the water would be love.

Commencement

Before the bee was scooped
into the car and hit me
in the thigh, so I let go
of the steering wheel,

we had been listening
to Seger, drinking Cokes,
talking about teachers
we would never see again,
the summer air washing
through the station wagon,
the summer sun assuring us
we could choose any direction
and end up somewhere great,

then we were arrowing
through an Indiana corn field
and Danny was screaming
JesusJesusJesusJesusJesus.

As the Poet Read a Poem about the First Time She Saw a Prostitute

As the poet read a poem about the first time she saw a prostitute,
a woman looking "so sassy" in purple and red, I remembered
a September afternoon, outside a Burger King in Wyoming,
my dad's blue Air Force duffel at my feet, when a girl
in jeans, tennis shoes, and grey sweat-shirt put her tray
at the next table, nodded, and asked, "How's it going?"
"Fine," I said, which was a lie. I was returning to school
reluctantly, unable to decide on a major, a life, but I said
"Fine. And you?" She shrugged, "Not bad." She ate
her fries. I started wondering what life would be like
if I had grown up in Cheyenne, or if I decided to stay now,
turning a forty-five minute stop into a defining moment.
I was trying to imagine possible careers I could have
when she asked, "How about it?" Afraid I had said "plumber"
or "sports reporter" out loud, I asked, "How about what?"
"Fifty dollars," she answered. I was shocked. I couldn't
loan her fifty dollars; we had just met and I didn't have a job.
Now I realize it took me so long because she didn't wear purple
or red, she didn't look sassy; she reminded me of Abigail,
a girl from Kansas who lived in my dorm. Finally something
about her voice or the tilt of her head made me realize what
the money was for, and I felt embarrassed not to have known
the minute she sat a little too close, proud at being solicited
like an adult, but mostly nervous. "Sorry," I said, grabbing
my bag, "I have to catch a bus." I walked away, ignoring her
question, "Where are you going?" Afterwards I never talked
easily with Abigail even as I stopped by her room more often,

and for years I forgot about that dented metal table covered
with cigarette marks, the acne spots on her cheeks, the way
the duffel hit my leg until a poet read a poem about a prostitute
and the smell of hamburgers, diesel, and longing filled the room.

On Looking at Frida Kahlo's *Little Deer*

i.

We notice the suffering, of course,
with its human face, the arrows
suggesting the cruelty, even sadism,
of whoever shot it again and again,
and we wonder at the attention
to detail, the painting of each piercing,
the insistence on her pain,
which evokes pity, then annoyance,
but eventually we begin to consider
other questions, like what animal
we would be. A bear? A lion?
Wouldn't it be better to be something
no one wants or bothers to hunt?

ii.

She shows her face and changes
her crippled body into a deer.
I would want the reverse. I would
give myself an elephant head,
not on this middle-aged sagging torso,
but on my younger chunky self,
the kid who wore Huskies and kept
his t-shirt on when swimming.
This is the power of art, to become
neither hunted, nor hunter,
but Ganesh, the elephant dancer,
the trickster, transforming the arrows
of outrageous fortune into incense sticks,
easily burned and casually swept away.

ACCIDENTS

Drivers

Although we don't want to, we have to stop to change
the baby, so we pull into a McDonalds, and afterwards
we let her crawl around as we drink coffee, eat fries,
and watch other people's children in the PlayPlace
fight over Ronald's car. A girl who wears a t-shirt
saying *Brat for Life* tries to drag *It IS all about me*
off the seat while *Spoiled Rotten Princess* waits
for a chance to swoop in. Before our child arrived,
we took turns in France driving a car as tiny as a toy
past indecipherable signs, but now I understand
at least the one at every roundabout which insists:
Vous n'avez pas priorité. It doesn't matter what
direction you're coming from, how smart, rich,
old, or beautiful you are. Whenever you approach
an intersection, you must yield in the presence of others.

Conversation

Daddy, what are these?
my three-year-old daughter asks,
pointing to the car grill
and the dozens of insects
we have smashed
while driving around.

I want to say "spots"
or "nothing" or
"I don't know."
I want to put off discussions
like this until she's older
or at least with her mother,
but I know I can't.

Bugs, I say, *Just bugs.*

Why are they there?

We hit them.

She knows this is bad;
a boy down the street
was hit by a car
and taken away
in an ambulance.

Should we take them
to the hospital?

No. They're dead.

We carry the bags
into the house
and unload the groceries.
Later, after dinner
and the evening bath,
we work on a puzzle.
As she tries
to figure out
how the sky
fits together,
she says
without turning around,

  They don't want to be dead,
  do they?

No, I say, *No, they don't.*

Baking with My Daughter

I want to do it, she says at each step
of the recipe, and I try to let her
even if it means broken eggs on the counter,
too much salt, and too little flour.

She splays the dough onto the cookie sheet,
using the wooden spoon as if it's a combination
snow shovel and mallet. When she turns away,
I try to perform a kind of cookie triage,
finding those blobs with a chance at survival
and nudging them into a vague roundness.

After they're finished, she holds one aloft
like a medal and tells her mother,
I did these all by myself, right Daddy?
I nod, saying nothing, and, for the first time,
wonder how many of my own victories
were smoothed into shape behind my back.

The Fist as a Unit of Measurement

In the book we read about the body,
one chapter explains, "The heart
is the size of a fist," and another says,
"The brain is the size of two fists."
So, as my daughter looks closely
at drawings of organs and bones,
I think about the fist as a unit
of measurement and wonder
if we should use it more often.
Recipes could call for a fist or two
of flour. I might shop for shoes
in my size of three and half fists.
Since we determine length by feet,
it makes sense to measure volume
this way, but however gratifying
it might be to have such a symbol
of force and grasping, I know
what would be lost, a sense of this
intimate distance, a parent and child,
lying together on a crumb-covered carpet,
her ten clenched fingers, her brain,
my five clenched fingers, my heart.

Edges

Before dawn, my son starts crying
at the top of the stairs, so I go up
and slide into his bed to keep him
quiet while his mother and sister sleep.
He struggles to get comfortable
on his belly, his side, his back,
finally calming with his head wedged
against my hip, as if trying to ram me
off the edge. Delicately balanced,
I watch the cows of his mobile
emerge in the changing light,
and with his breath pulsing
into my side as regular as iambs,
I remember lines of your poems
and wonder where you are now.
Do you have children? Are you
writing? I had thought our lives
would interweave like lines
of a sestina, moving together
and apart through the stanzas
of decades, the repetition of jobs,
marriages, kids, no less pleasurable
for their obvious fixed patterns,
but instead I find my life consists
of a juxtaposition of fragments,
cries for comfort from ones
who cannot speak, shards of poems
left by those who choose not to.

Shaking Hands

When we arrive, he's there, as always,
standing on the porch like a sentinel,
watching as we unfold ourselves
from the car after hours on the road.
I climb the steps, he reaches out,
and for the first time I notice his hands
tremble, but then he has me locked
in that familiar firm clasp, the one
he taught me years ago, insisting
I do it over and over as he explained
the importance of first impressions,
how a handshake reveals something
about strength, confidence, trust, all
you need to know about a person.
As he asks about the weather and trip,
I turn towards my son and remind him
what we were practicing in the car,
so he climbs the steps, holds up
his two-year-old fingers, and shouts,
"How'd do! How'd do!" Solemn
as a priest, my father shakes hands,
then begins laughing hard enough
to attract the neighbors' attention,
and as he hoists his grandson
above his head, I assure myself
that what I had seen must have been
an illusion, the result of road fatigue,
some failing, some weakness of mine.

Inheritance

My father asks what I'll want
when he's dead. He plans
to have everything auctioned
and the money split among
his children, but each of us
can mark pieces to save.

There is so much in his house
that I don't want, yet I know
I have to choose something
or be seen as rejecting all
he has gathered in his life.
As we tour the rooms, I think

of Wheel of Fortune, how
at the end, people searched
for things to spend the last
of their money on. *I guess
I'll take the ceramic dogs
for two hundred, Jack.*

I look for something. Finally
I say, "Dad, what I'll want
when you're dead is for you
to not be dead." He's touched.
He hugs me, and then he says,
"But what else? What else?"

Alignment

Because the road to the daycare goes east,
on spring mornings we drive towards the sun
along a corridor of flowering dogwoods,
and it may be the illuminated white petals,
the second coffee I had before we left,
or Pink doing a Steve Miller song, the one
from *Happy Feet* that made me realize
she has a great voice, but suddenly I'm close
to tears. I have to lock my elbows to keep
the van on the road. Then I start laughing
because of how difficult it would be to explain
I drove into a tree after being overwhelmed
by the enigmatic beauty of this world.
From the backseat, my son asks, "Daddy,
What's wrong?" and when I say, "Nothing,
I'm just happy," he claps, "I'm happy too!"

Love Me Do

Each morning as I take my son to day-care,
before we even reach the car, he insists,
"Beatles, Daddy, Beatles!" But I can't
slide in just any Fab Four cd. The work after
Rubber Soul evokes cries of "Don't like it!"
and foot stamps against the seat which is
unfortunate because his whistle and drum,
his yells of "Let's go!" and "Red light!"
fit with "Yellow Submarine" and most
of *Sgt Pepper* and *Magical Mystery Tour*.
He prefers the early cuts, especially those
from *Meet the Beatles*. After hearing
these hundreds of times, I feel I'm finally
listening. Each week I notice something
different: how Ringo is working his ass off
on "She Loves You," Lennon's rough voice
on "Twist and Shout," the way those *wooo*s
in "I Want to Hold Your Hand" which some
seem to consider the last cry of innocence
before the beards and velvet coats, are really
the pressure whistles of boilers. Each song
is a celebration at finding a form to hold
their energy. No wonder my son likes them;
he knows about primal emotions, how hard
they are to master, the way exuberance
melds with impatience, and the rough joy
of banging noise into shapes with people
you love, almost in control and almost out.

30

Accidents

It was an accident, my daughter says
to explain yet another spill or why
her younger brother's crying upstairs.
It was an accident, she yells so soon
after the crash it seems all one sound.
She carries the word like a shield,
a get-out-jail free card, a safe base,
protecting her from any punishment.
After all, when accidents happen,
no one's responsible. I try to explain
when a glass falls after she's put it on top
of the stepstool on top of the chair on top
of the couch, she can't call it an accident.
But, even as we talk about how our actions
may have unanticipated results, I recognize
the appeal of her position, and I wonder
how much of it we could adopt. Why not
consider disappointing dinner parties,
bad gifts, awkward kisses, as accidents?
Every horoscope could read, "Today,
you will be involved in an accident."
Headstones could have the inscription,
It was an accident, an explanation,
not of how we died, but how we lived,
the way our curiosity and desire resulted
in breakage, odd collisions, lives full
of consequences, mostly unintended.

Curbs

My children play in the leaves piled at the curb.
They dive, fall, somersault, hurl themselves
with the abandon of those who have never
run into a door in the dark. Watching them,
I try not to think of sharp branches underneath,
how in grade school we told a story about a boy
who jumped into hay that had a pitchfork in it
and the tines speared underwear into his guts,
how one winter Mike shattered his eye socket
when he drove a snowmobile into a drift
covering a fire hydrant. My kids bury themselves
in the leaves, and I try not to think of John and me
drinking beer and gunning his Dodge Charger
into garbage cans, mailboxes, saplings, bushes,
piles of leaves. I stand in the road, a sentinel,
curbing the possibilities, yet careful to smile
whenever a head pops up like a curious seal
to make sure I'm there appreciating all this fun.

The Watch

I tell my children we'll stay for one hour,
and as they run from the swings to the slides
to the monkey bars, he walks over and sits
next to me. We watch my daughter climb
a platform, and, just as she leans for a pole,
she becomes distracted, so she almost steps
into nothingness. *Be careful,* I yell. She looks
over with a familiar expression of annoyance.
Be careful, I repeat, and he laughs. *You can't
watch them all the time and even if you could,
I'll get them eventually.* I say nothing, but think,
Not today, please, not today, and when I realize
he's begun looking at the other children, I feel
ashamed at my sense of relief, but still relieved.

Beacon

The other campsites all have large fires,
ones you can see burning from far away.
Ours is modest, a few logs, a small flame.
Maybe it's because of the Westerns I read
as a kid that warned a big fire draws attention,
dulls the senses, *will get you killed*, or maybe
it's guilt at having any fire when we don't
need its warmth or light. We're not using it
to cook, but even though my children have
never been camping, they know the ritual
elements we must have: tent, sleeping bags,
flashlights, fire. A drunk guy from the site
that's been playing classic rock since lunch
stumbles up, stares, then says, "Hey. Hey!"
I stand, move closer to the children, grip
a piece of kindling. "If you used your air
mattress pump on that, you'd get it going.
It would light it up like a goddamn torch."
I thank him for the tip. As he crashes away,
it occurs to me the other sites have been
pitying us, the sad family hunched around
the meager flames. I feel a flash of anger,
a desire to show I can provide, to prove
I can get things burning. It's a sentiment
unworthy of a Mountain Man, Jim Bridger,
Kit Carson, Hugh Glass, Jedediah Smith,
but I don't remember them having kids.

I throw the stick into the circle, and ask,
"Does anyone here want a bigger fire?"
"Yeah!" the children shout, a response
I suspect they would give if I asked
whether we should set the woods ablaze.
Then my wife says in the voice she uses
when suggesting maybe I shouldn't wear
that particular shirt again, "It might be nice
to have a fire that's more like a fire."
Stoked, I go to the tent and find the pump.
The drunk is right; it works like a torch,
a goddamn torch, and soon I have flames
that delight my family, burn brightly
in the night, serve as a beacon to illuminate
who I am and what I am willing to do.

Burning Down the House

My daughter wants to know
if she can have a "baby fire"
to take care of. She promises,
"I won't let it get out, and
I'll call 9-1-1-1-1 if it does."
I'm tempted to say, "I never
got to have a fire at your age,"
but she might not get the joke,
or understand it's not a joke.
Before I was born, my brother
and sister decided to build
a fire in the living room.
They lit paper on the stove,
but only made it to the hall
before dropping the flame.
My parents liked to tell how,
at hearing screaming, they ran
in to find a fire on the stairs;
each time I didn't hear concern,
but laughter and wonder, until
I regretted never having tried
to set the house on fire myself,
never having come so close
to tragedy they loved me more.
I was the youngest, the one
who came along after the family
was already a family, the one

who never destroyed anything,
but who secretly wanted to,
which may be why I ended up
burning so much in my life,
people and opportunities,
money and time and bridges.
Maybe my daughter would be
happier later if I let her play
with fire now? Maybe it would
burn a ring of safety around her.
Maybe for her next birthday,
I will get her a baby fire
instead of Princess Barbie.
It will teach her responsibility,
to be careful with her desires,
how much I love her, how much
I want her to have more than I did.

Thickening

As I learned to cook, I discovered
the magical qualities of heat,
how it creates gravies and sauces,
changing liquid into something more
substantial right before our eyes.
Standing at the stove, I would repeat
"thickening" as if it was a spell,
an incantation, and, in the kitchen,
the word delights. Who doesn't love
thick shakes? Thick slices of bread?

But in the bedroom, at the mirror,
the word comes unbidden to describe
a body changing into something more
substantial right before my eyes,
perhaps because of those sauces,
or, perhaps this is the magical quality
of aging, how we're brought to boil,
then, through the years, continue
to simmer, thickening and thickening,
until our flavors become concentrated.

Easter Sunday

After I come back from a long run,
my wife sends me to the grocery
for fresh garlic, pears, more wine,
a good loaf of bread. There, I help
myself to samples, a cookie, a coffee,
and balancing these, I slackly steer
the cart with an elbow until I encounter
an old lady blocking the produce aisle.

In black church clothes, she squints
at something cupped in her hands.
At first, I think it's a list or a recipe
then I realize it's a small bible.
I see her again in the baking section,
her face still inches from the book,
nothing in her cart. The third time
I realize she's near, right behind me,

in the checkout lane, I'm tempted
to reach out and make sure she isn't
some figment risen from a childhood
I thought had been sealed off long ago,
an admonishment for my spending
this day as a contented animal,
unshaven, unshriven, piling up
a cart of this world's pleasures.

The End of the World

While everyone was waiting for the end of the world,
I was trying to find my keys, writing a grocery list,
and reminding myself to reschedule a dentist appointment.
I was taking the garbage out and stopping to marvel

at the half moon and the smell of wood smoke
from some neighbor's fire. I was watching a movie
with my wife on the couch, our legs intertwined,
and afterwards brushing, flossing, and going to bed.

The next morning we went to work, everyone and I,
they, ambivalent, thankful for the reprieve and yet
suspicious there was nothing to be reprieved from,
I, oblivious, wondering where I had left my list.

A Midnight Call About The End of the World

She calls to ask if it was the end of the world
what would I do. I know she wants to hear
something like "Run to you," "Crank up
REM and dance," or "Sing while drinking
champagne," but the streets would be packed,
Michael Stipe makes me too self-conscious
about my body, and I can never remember
lyrics. Champagne, however, might be okay
since I actually enjoyed a New Year's Eve
once, standing on a friend's roof, swigging
Moet & Chandon from a bottle and yelling
at people below who were yelling up at us.
That seems as good a way as any to face
the end, and if it's going to involve some sort
of visuals I could set up the lawn furniture
I bought years ago at Goodwill which, I think,
is in the basement somewhere, although
the bulb's burnt-out down there, so I'd need
a flashlight. Trying to imagine the sequence,
I must mumble something because she asks,
"What?" and I explain, "I'd have to find
a flashlight to go into the basement." At this,
she gives a small, mournful, "Oh," then says
nothing else, and, after a moment, I realize
she's hung up, and I'm standing in a dark room
holding a blinking cell phone, wondering
if I should call back, go to bed, or have a drink
on the porch, and then I recognize this may be
exactly what the end of the world will be like.

My Dream Self

Lately I've been disappointed in my dream self
who seems to be coasting, wasting his talents
and opportunities. For someone who can create
worlds where people can fly, be invisible, walk
through walls, die and return, speak all languages
including imaginary ones, why does he spend
his time on this doggerel? What's the point
of yet another teaching anxiety dream? Or
the endless running? The friends who pretend
not to see me? Once being naked in a food court
might have been evocative, now it doesn't
even earn a shrug. There is blood, of course;
there's always blood, but too often it feels
compulsory, a requirement of the Dream Union.
It's as if he's just going through the motions
until retirement. There hasn't been anything
fresh in years. Nothing like the volleyball game
with Princess Diana or the glowing mobile grave
always following a few feet behind. Perhaps
he has other things on his mind, moonlighting
jobs, family concerns. Whatever the situation is,
he could do so much more with what he has,
but then, I suppose, he says the same about me.

Another Morning After

On some mornings
our preparations
resemble a waltz
as we move in tandem
around the house,
showering and shaving,
making toast and tea,
pouring cereal
and preparing lunches,
a complex choreography
we've worked out
over the years.

On other days,
we stumble, off
step, off
balance, colliding,
unable to
anticipate the other's
moves, unsure
of our own
direction.

Then there are
times like this
when, as I pour juice,
milk, and coffee,

and she spreads jelly
across the bread
in just the thickness
our daughter likes,
the radio gives
yet another report
on the aftermath,
and I realize she's crying.

I stop and touch
her bathrobe so lightly
I don't know if she can
even feel it, and she says,
I don't want them
to go anywhere.
I don't want them
to leave the house.

For a moment we stand
next to one another,
then we continue the steps
that will take us through
another unstoppable day.

Night Questions

She calls them "night questions," the ones we consider
after we've staked the tents, put the children to bed,
and eaten a meal that reassures us we're safe for a while.
Like stars, invisible in the luminosity of the day's obligations,
they emerge after dusk and brighten with the wine and fire.
Some we return to again and again, using them to orient
ourselves. Others form into constellations of myth and song,
delight and desire. A few comfort us with a familiar constancy,
linking the past and future. Then there are those, we hesitate
to acknowledge, the ones that make us zip up our jackets
and pull our blankets tighter, the ones we fear can never be
answered, the ones we know can only be answered by howling
at the moon, the sea, and the trackless darkness in between.

Stackables

In the department store, the package
for a wooden toy train trumpets: "Cars
Are Stackable!" and I'm puzzled by this
selling point since the appeal of a train
is horizontal, but then I notice the word
everywhere. Dishes, lawn furniture,
chairs, tables, bookshelves, jewelry,
bins, boxes, washers, dryers, all can be
stacked, and I circle the bright displays
with the same puzzled awe I've felt
browsing San Francisco's Columbarium,
whose windowed niches showcase
urns, mementoes, names, and I think
of us, how we've spent so many nights
sliding onto one another, how efficient
we are in our design, our lives stackable,
fitting together with no top and no bottom.

How You Know

How do you know if it's love? my daughter asks,
and I think if you have to ask, it's not,
but I know this won't help. I want to say
you're too young to worry about it,
as if she has questions about Medicare
or social security, but this won't help either.
"You'll just know" is a lie, and one truth,
"when you still want to be with them
the next morning" would involve too
many follow-up questions. The difficulty
with love, I want to say, is sometimes
you only know afterwards that it's arrived
or left. Love is the elephant and we
are the blind mice unable to understand
the whole. I want to say love is this
desire to help even when I know I can't,
just as I couldn't explain electricity, stars,
the color of the sky, baldness, tornadoes,
fingernails, coconuts, or the other things
she has asked about over the years, all
those phenomenon whose daily existence
seems miraculous. Instead I shake my head.
I don't even know how to match my socks.
Go ask your mother. She laughs and says,
I did. Mom told me to come and ask you.

WHERE WE ARE NOW

On My Mother's 70th Birthday

After I sing "Happy Birthday," I identify myself,
and we talk about the weather, where I live now,
how clear the phone signal is, what the bill might be.
When I mention her age again, I feel the confusion.
70? That can't be right. There has been a mistake.
She has been cheated somehow of time owed to her.
How old are you? she asks in a tone that suggests
her suspicion I'm in on the con, then she demands
the ages of my brother, sister, wife and children.
With each answer, I can sense a growing anger
at this betrayal by her family, who, behind her back,
have grown older than the woman she knows she is.

The Comfort of Family

My mother begins to cry because she's alone,
having grown up with no brothers or sisters.
It's a sentiment I've never heard before,
and, I guess, it's reassuring to know,
even at seventy, you still can develop
fresh ways to make yourself feel like shit.

I point out, siblings don't always get along.
Doesn't she remember how her children fought?
She says, *That's just because you were all mean
to each other. You are just so dog-gone mean.*

I insist she's not alone. She has family
and friends who visit, who call, who care.
She says, *Whatever*, gives a dismissive wave,
and turns away, annoyed by my obstinacy,
my refusal to admit that she didn't get
all the people she deserved from this life.

Correspondence

I would recognize the handwriting
on each manila envelope and know
the contents without opening it,
more photocopies of photographs
she had already sent several times,
including one from twenty years ago
of me standing in my dorm room,
long hair, smirk, hands on my hips.
Across my chest, she would write
with fat marker "J-O-E." A post-it
would say something like, "You might
get a kick out of these." I never did.
Instead I found them annoying, mainly
because I looked fat and vacuous.
I wanted to forget who I used to be,
and she kept reminding me, but now
I realize those envelopes indicated
something was wrong, and my name
in big letters wasn't a mother offering
helpful notations to future historians,
but an attempt to keep her family
clearly labeled and firmly in place.

My Brother Stands Behind a One-Way Window Looking at My Mother Trying to Convince the Psychiatrist to Release Her by Talking and Acting the Way She Thinks Other People Might Consider Normal While I Eat Lunch at a Wendy's and Read the Letters of Seneca

As I finish my french fries,
I look out the window
and notice a traffic light
is broken, and people are trying
to figure out who gets to go
next and if the others agree.
Sometimes the cars rotate
in an obvious order,
and sometimes someone
guns through the intersection
because of impatience or ignorance
or arrogance. I suspect
some textbook suggests
the systems of behavior
that govern us at these moments,
or there are people
who can explain how
we deal with break-downs
in our daily lives,
but I find myself wanting
to do my own study
and catch each car
before it accelerates away
to survey what people have
beside them. How many

have daytimers, palm pilots,
cell phones, hospital numbers
scribbled on paper scraps?
How many carry maps,
directions, first aid kits?
I could collect the data,
collate the statistics,
arrange the results
in pie charts and bar graphs,
showing in clear categories
something about the way
we travel and what we keep
near us: fast food wrappers,
pills, cigarettes, coffee cups,
paperback books that offer
advice on how to live
by people who died long ago.

Where We Are Now

Walking along the seashore,
we stop for water and chocolate.
I watch waves cover and uncover
sand and rocks. She looks
at the map, even though the trail
is only a couple of well marked miles,
and with the ocean on one side,
it's impossible to get lost. This is
what she always does. Each hike,
trip, and visit must be charted
before, during, and after. She asks
everyone she meets to show her
on the atlas she always carries
where they're from and what route
has taken them to her. As I scan
the horizon for whales, even though
it's not migration season, she says
"I know where we are now," pointing
to a spot on the map. "We're here.
We're right here." I shake my head,
"No, Mom," then sweep my arm
in a circle. "We're here. Right here."

I will tell this story many times,
smugly satisfied by how it shows
I know what's important, but later
it will become clear I've misread

her obsession, considering it a joke,
an annoyance, instead of a symptom,
a sign that for years, maybe most
of her life, she has been trying
to keep from getting lost, trying
to locate her place in the world,
trying to figure out where she is,
how she got there, how to get home.

Her Story

For years my mother would talk
about the book she would write
for children when she had the time
(although she would often point out
she had never wanted to have kids).
It was about the big yellow semi
she owned and used for long hauls,
and she called it the Banana Rama
Truckeroo Story, or sometimes
the Banana Rama Truckeroo Series.
She would call to ask my advice
about the marketing, the TV show,
the merchandising, if I thought
Clint Eastwood might be right
for the voice of the animated version
or if she should go with someone
younger like Brad Pitt or Matt Damon.
She would call to ask how she could
get an agent, an advance, how much
she would get in royalties, how to keep
her ideas from being stolen. Each day
she would call several times, always
with the same questions, and I could see
how it would be at the end with her
only being able to say "banana banana"
or "roo roo" over and over, leaving me
to explain to a puzzled nursing staff,
"That's her story, the story of her life."

Collisions

I can drive with my eyes closed
she yells, as we have the red car
she's owned for years towed away.
We have stopped trying to explain
that it isn't safe—she isn't safe—
but she continues to insist, *It's not*
fair. I've never had an accident.
She must see something in our faces
because before we can recite the list
or even offer our favorite examples,
like the Christmas she called from jail
after hitting someone without knowing it
or the time her truck caught fire and
she kept driving until they had to shut
the highway down, she adds, *In that car!*
Those times in that car, they hit me
while I was sitting at intersections!
This could be a summary of her life.
She was in control and minding
her own business when others,
always it was others, collided into her.

The Road

We have been trying to let her
stay at home as long as possible,
calling in shifts to remind her
to take her pills and eat, sometimes
talking her through a meal,
but when the machine picks up
for the third day in a row we know
something is wrong. My brother
goes over after work, half-expecting
to find a body, but instead there is
nothing. No one. The neighbors
explain they saw my mother walk
away, or, rather, ride away, climbing
into the cab of a semi that's often
been parked in the neighborhood.

We think we met the driver
months ago when he visited her
at the hospital during her evaluation
period. An old high school friend
he had said, mumbling a name
none of us had heard before.
The nurses told us later that despite
his wedding ring *they sat too close*
to be cousins. We started calling him
"The Silver Fox" and wondered how
he had known where to find her.

None of us remember his name,
so all we can do is wait and ask,
"What is he thinking?" It's clear
she's unwell, but that may be
the appeal. She will forget
he's married, no matter how often
he confesses. We wonder if
he's a predator, in denial, or
just wants one last ride together.

As for her, having spent years
on the road *driving truck*,
swinging up into the cab
must have felt reassuring,
almost like coming home,
and it must be comforting
to wake up next to someone
in that familiar smell of diesel,
metal, vinyl, and rubber,
believing that he cares
enough to take her away
rather than lock her up.

I find myself hoping
they're on a long run,
and that she doesn't notice
when he finally makes
the inevitable turn to bring her
back home, back to her family,
back to our loving, crushing care.

Taking His Place

My mother becomes furious
each time she hears the diagnosis.

My mother died of cancer.
My father died of cancer.
I was supposed to get cancer.

I want to point out cancer
isn't a birthright, or something
to regret not getting, but I know
this would only make her madder.

After all the times I prayed for this
not to happen. After all the times
I went to church when I didn't
want to go, when I had other things
to do. After all the things I've done
for him, God has betrayed me.

I want to ask if she had anything in writing.
Did God sign a contract, or was it only
an oral agreement? Did she at least
get a handshake? And what about
the other seven million with the disease?
What did she think their agreements
with him had been? Perhaps they could
file some sort of class action grievance.

I asked to be hit by a car, taken
in my sleep, have someone kill me,
but not this. I didn't ask for this.
It isn't fair. It Is Not Fair!

I've learned not to argue with this
accusation of betrayal. I've heard it
about my father and her father,
her second husband, my brother,
myself, her bosses and co-workers,
her friends, relatives, and neighbors.
The fact is God is just
taking his place in the long line
of assholes who have failed her,
and we know better than to try
to stick up for one another.

Fallen Timbers

The courthouse is across from Lincoln Life,
the insurance building where she worked
forty years ago as she raised the three kids
who now *want to put me away!*
In prison! After all I've been through
they want to put me in prison!
Built in a Beaux Arts style when people
still believed in monumental grandeur
and the beauty of the law, its windows
suggest transparency, its multiple doors,
accessibility, but now our sense of justice
has been reduced, and everyone files
through a single narrow entrance,
a security checkpoint stripping us
of our phones, BlackBerrys, iPods, all
modern life's dangerous weaponry.

Inside, scaffolding and plastic sheeting
cover the walls. Exhibition panels explain
the renovations underway. Photos detail
the damage the years have done, particularly,
to the murals depicting the "dreadful figures
of Death, Pestilence and Devastation" and
the one of the Battle of Fallen Timbers,
where in a forest ripped apart by a tornado
Little Turtle met the Revolutionary General
Mad Anthony Wayne for the third time.
Twice before, the Miami chief had stopped

"the nation's westward movement,"
but the insurgent fighting for his freedom
finally lost to the man who fought like crazy.
In fourth grade, I played General Wayne,
and I was supposed to tell Little Turtle
that, although I respected him, his way
of life was over, and I would crush him
if he resisted me. When the curtain rose,
I went for laughs, mugging and warning
him not to mess with me because I was nuts.
Todd kept turning to Mrs. Brooks, hoping
she would step in, but I remember thinking
she couldn't interfere once the play
had started and that the design on his shirt
looked nothing like a turtle, at least
not the ones my brother would catch
at my grandfather's lake cottage.
He would spend the day scooping
snappers and box turtles from the water,
painting numbers on their shells then
letting them crawl back to the lake,
which seems similar to what the doctor
suggested as we reviewed our options
about what to do with our mother.
He called it "the libertarian approach,"
letting her go to fend for herself.
Like setting her loose in the woods,
I suggested, but no one laughed.

We finally find the probate court
at the end of a long hallway. Small
with fluorescent lights and hard pews
like a strip mall church, it has

nothing on its walls, no paintings,
no murals, no history. We stand
when the judge enters. He wears
a yellow LiveStrong bracelet, the only
color in the room, and since he seems
about our age, I wonder whether
we could have gone to school together
and if he ever recognizes families
in front of him. Where is Todd now?
Mrs. Brooks? Then we begin, giving
testimony about the mind that has had
a series of tornados sweep through it,
describing our battles in its ruins.

Cleaning Out the House

I pitch the box of Trojans I find on the top closet shelf
and keep the Virginia Slims from the back of a drawer.

I drink the Slimfast shakes, eat the SnackWell cookies,
and try not to imagine what her reaction would be

if she came back and saw the heaped bags of clothes,
the furniture by a "Free" sign, the boxed up self-help books,

the son who had never visited those years she lived here,
smoking the pack she had been saving for a special occasion.

Inscriptions

She put her name on everything,
coats, gloves, shoes, shirts,
tools, books, dishes, clocks,
luggage, printer, stapler, hoses,
sprinklers, flashlights, buckets.
Sometimes she included a heart
or smiley face among the fat
black or blue lettering, but mostly
it was her name again and again.
At first I thought this was to deter
thieves or make sure loaned items
were returned, but that didn't
explain the name on underwear,
flower pots, the water heater cover,
then I wondered, if, like a child,
she was asserting her presence,
her ego—*mine, mine, mine, mine,
mine.* Finally I realized that despite
the crucifix on the wall (with
her name written on the bottom),
these were spells, incantations,
attempts to create a magic ring
of protection and preservation
by claiming the pieces of this
world were not only hers but her.

Waiters

My mother is afraid the flowers we've given her
to leave will blow away, so I search the plots
for branches to stake the bouquet into the ground.
My brother says a prayer. My sister points out
grandpa was twenty years older than his wife.
Not bad, she laughs. We ask what the initials
on the headstones stand for, and Mom squints
at the chiseled letters, but doesn't say anything.
We spend an hour browsing the other graves
as if we're in a thrift store uncovering oddities,
Hey, did you see this? Come check this out.
Then we go to a nearby restaurant none of us
particularly likes.
                   We insist, *Get anything*
you want, Mom, but it's as if she's never seen
a menu and can't figure out how it works.
The waiter suggests the special, and she looks
at him with suspicion. She's heard eggplant
is purple. Why would she eat something purple?
My sister orders pasta for her. When it comes,
she pokes around the noodles with a fork
as if the plate has been booby-trapped.
We try to reassure her—*You'll like it*—
but she shakes her head and clenches her lips.
Later the waiter offers a box for leftovers,
and even she laughs.

We knew it would be
difficult to move her from the house and all
her familiar routines, and we knew it might
be uncomfortable having her rely on us after
she's been living alone for so long, but none
of us really understood how it would be
having to watch what she has get cleared away,
dish by dish, until she sits at an empty table,
unable to remember what meal it was
she didn't order, didn't want, didn't eat.

Singing to the Woman Who Used to Be My Mother

We bring our guitars to her room.
She's delighted and asks,
When did you learn to play guitar?
even though I've had one
since high school. She repeats
this question over and over
and over, and it becomes hard
to resist the temptation to answer,
In jail. When I was riding the rails
during the Depression. Guitar?
What do you mean? What guitar?

The music gives us something
to do, but my repertoire is limited,
consisting mainly of blues songs
about leaving, jumping in the river,
putting your head on the tracks,
being down and out and depressed,
subjects that might not be the best
for a suicidal woman with dementia.
I also know some Hank Williams,
but I don't think, "I'm so lonesome
I could die," or "I'll never get out
of this world alive," is any better,
although "Why don't you love me
like you used to do" seems appropriate.

My brother strums a familiar rhythm,
my mother begins clapping her hands,
and he starts singing "Folsom Prison Blues."
I give him a look to ask, "What the hell
are you doing?" but she doesn't connect
her prison with that prison.
When she hears he shot a man
in Reno just to watch him die,
she stops moving. Her face puckers.
That's not very nice, she says.
No, we agree, it's not very nice.
People can be mean, she says,
and starts to cry. Yes, we say,
then I begin playing a Beatles tune,
one of the early, peppy ones;
she smiles, taps her feet, and asks,
When did you learn to play guitar?

The Guardian

I don't think my brother realized all
the responsibilities involved in being
her guardian, not just the paperwork
but the trips to the dentist and Wal-Mart,
the making sure she has underwear,
money to buy Pepsis, the crying calls
because she has no shampoo even though
he has bought her several bottles recently.
We talk about how he might bring this up
with the staff, how best to delicately ask
if they're using her shampoo on others
or maybe just allowing her too much.
"You only need a little, Mom," he said,
"Not a handful." "I don't have any!"
she shouted before hanging up. Later
he finds a bottle stashed in her closet
and two more hidden in the bathroom
along with crackers, spoons, and socks.
Afraid, someone might steal her things,
she hides them, but then not only forgets
where but that she ever had them at all.

I tease my brother, "You always wanted
another kid." He doesn't laugh. She hated
her father, and, in this second childhood,
she resents the one who takes care of her.
When I call, she complains about how

my brother treats her and how she hasn't
seen him in years. If I explain everything
he's doing, she admires the way I stick up
for him. Doing nothing means I do nothing
wrong. This is love's blindness and love's
injustice. It's why I expect to hear anger
or bitterness in my brother's voice, and why
each time we talk, no matter how closely
I listen, I'm astonished to hear only love.

The Husband

He comes every day to eat lunch and sit
with her in the sun room. Sometimes he reads
letters out loud from their children or friends;
sometimes he reads the paper as she sleeps.
One day the staff makes her favorite cake
to celebrate their anniversary,
and he tells how, to buy her ring, he worked
months of overtime at the factory,
so she thought he was seeing someone else.
"As if I would look at other women
when I have Pearl," he says, shaking his head.
She begins to cry and tells him, "You're sweet,
but I miss my husband." He pats her hand.
"I know," he says, "It's all right. Try some cake."

Love Is

In high school, Cathy covered her locker
with "Love Is…" cartoons. They showed
little naked couples, holding hands,
looking at sunsets, flowers, one another.
None of them suggested the smell
of cleansers and aerosol sprays.
None of the hands were palsied.
None of the sunsets were seen from
behind windows that couldn't be opened
more than three inches. But, this is
probably as it should be. Art is not
always the lie that tells the truth;
sometimes it's the lie that helps us
deal with the truth. Of what good is
knowing what's to come or where
love will lead us? Still, if I knew
Cathy's address now, I might send her
the email Sean wrote from Alabama
where he has gone to try to find
a place that will take his father.
It mentions he's tired, it's hot, and
"sometimes love is just showing up."

Working on the Office

In her last years, each time I called
she would be working on her office,
sorting files and correspondence,
and we would agree it was amazing
how paperwork accumulated.
I would sympathize and joke,
but also wonder how she could
be working on the office yet again.
Later, when I have to clear it out,
I better understand the difficulty
of the task because she had made
multiple files and notes to herself,
copies of letters to her lawyer,
her accountant, her hairdresser,
her bosses, her mechanic, her doctor,
her dentist, her phone company,
seemingly everyone with whom
she had some type of contact,
and these consisted of detailed
complaints, chronicling her sense
of betrayal at what she considered
unfulfilled promises. Each threatened
to pursue legal action unless she
received some type of satisfaction.
Trying to sort through the file cabinets,
drawers, and storage boxes full

of documentation about how people
had failed her, I become unsure
which papers might be important.
What if I throw out evidence
for some pending suit? I begin
putting more and more folders aside
to deal with next week, or month,
or year, hoping they will make sense
later when I work on the office again.

The Loss of Paris

We'll always have Paris
Bogey tells her, and we want
to believe him because this
insistence on a portable world,
which can never be taken away,
makes partings bearable,
but eventually, we realize
the faces of lovers fade,
details we thought we would
remember fall from us
like scraps of paper.
Vacations, jobs, years,
friends disappear.
In the end, we always have
nothing, not even the consolation
of believing we will remember,
and all we can hope for
is forgetting we expected to.

LEARNING TO FALL

A Road Labeled "F-E-A-R"

What do you fear? my students ask,
and I think, "Whatever you say
can be used against you," and I think,
"The ingenuity of students to turn
me away from my prepared lesson,"
and I think, "One of you making headlines
with a gun," and I think, "My children
having children too early or drinking
and driving or doing the stupid things
I did growing up," but I decide to admit
how I used to be afraid that as I crossed
the street, a car would go past and slice
off my kneecaps. I don't worry about it
as much now that fenders are smooth
and molded, no gaps, no edges, but that's
also why it's hard for them to understand,
so I draw a diagram on the board, chalking
a car with old-fashioned bumpers on a road
labeled "F-E-A-R." A stick figure stands
wide-eyed, hands hovering over huge knees.
One student contemplates the sketch
then says, "They'd have to get really close."
Yes, I nod, that's it, that's exactly what I fear,
the crippling closeness of people passing by.

Cutters

When she raises her hand, I try to look at her eyes
rather than the raised ridges vining along her arms,
the scars that show she's a cutter, or was once,
but I know they're there, and I think of my daughter
wanting to help in the kitchen and grabbing a blade,
how in school we played "bloody knuckles," smashing
cards onto our hands until they bled and sometimes
sliding one from the pack so it slit like a razor, and
all those nights drinking, driving, throwing our bodies
around like airline luggage. Someone once told me,
What a person needs in this world is a sharp knife
and the will to use it, as if the problems of our lives
were Gordian knots, each solvable with a quick slice.
I used to believe it. But now, when my student's arm
rises, I call on her, even if other hands are already up,
as if my attention could bind, at least for a moment,
the damage we do to ourselves we can never cut away.

Learning to Fall

"I think today we're learning to fall,"
one girl tells her friend who has asked
what they'll be doing in drama class,
and I'm tempted to say, "That's funny.
We're doing that in here too" because
even though teachers pretend to train
artists, scientists, modern Daedaluses,
our job, despite what the brochures
and course catalogues say, is not
to teach them how to fly, but fall.

Each of us is an Icarus with
the only question being how far
we'll get before the inevitable
descent and whether we'll survive.
But, I say only, "Let's get started"
and begin writing on the board
as they groan, pull out books,
brace themselves for questions
that will tumble them earthward.

Among School Children

Walking to class, I hear a girl say,
"That's our post-coital hangout."
I resist turning to see who's speaking
although I'm not surprised by the sex
or public talk of it. At a campus film,
someone behind me told her friend
(and everyone within a dozen rows),
she was living her life by the credo,
"There's always room for Jell-O,
and there's always time for sex."

No, what surprises me is how casually
the girl has used the Latin "post-coital,"
and even though I may be indifferent
to what she does with her body,
I confess I'm titillated by her vocabulary.

As I step into my classroom and write
the day's assignment on the board,
I think of my wife, and where, before
she was my wife, we would hang out,
drinking pot after pot of tea, speaking
to one another in various languages,
the joy on our tongues new and ancient.

Casting

A student stops by my office to say
he missed class because he was
auditioning for *As the World Turns,*
which is also why his work will be late;
in fact, he doesn't know if he can do
much of anything until he finds out.
I'm surprised to realize he's not there
to apologize or see what he missed,
but simply explain. Rising to leave,
he says, "Pray for me, Professor."
It's a brilliant tactic, one that pulls me
off balance, because I've braced myself
against an extension request or plea
for extra credit since he's missed much
more than just a week. For a moment
I consider possible ways to respond.
Should I point out if he came to class
more he might know I'm not the type
to pray? And, even if I was, I would
probably be economical in my requests,
so it's doubtful I would use one to try
to land a student a role on a soap.
But maybe he knows this. Maybe it's
a dead-pan joke, an ironic put-on.
After all, he is an actor. Perhaps
I've failed to recognize a complex wit
behind that beautiful B-movie face,

but, no, even after years of training,
he can't control his emotions, his awe
at life's amazing opportunities,
his excitement at the adventures
ahead. His sincerity and belief
I care as much as he does makes me
feel old and irritable. I'm annoyed
with him, with myself, with the way
we keep swallowing those hooks
that always, no matter how they look,
have the same bait: "This is yours
because you're special." I want
to warn him not to bite too hard,
to say the best that I can hope for
him is a director, a boss, a lover
who practices catch and release.
Instead I hold up crossed fingers,
that secular equivalent of prayer
and say, "Good luck. Let me know
how it turns out. And, please, try
to get me your work as soon as you can."

Dispersal

As my student reads a poem about dandelions,
I think about how this spring my five-year-old
has turned each walk into a dandelion hunt.
She gathers the yellow ones into bouquets,
but she prizes the white puffs most. Seeing one
she sprints to it as if afraid someone else
will get there first, then she carries it back
to me before blowing. How old was I when
Mrs. Turner, who lived alone, started screaming
"Stop it! Stop that!" at seeing me whistle
white seeds into the air, as if I was the one
responsible for ruining her yard and her life?

We used to ask each other, "Do you like butter"
as we rubbed the yellow flowers on our chins,
or we would flick them from the stems, singing,
"Momma had a baby and her head popped off."
My college RA made dandelion wine and played
music by the great stride pianist Willy the Lion.
When the student finally finishes, I want to say,
"Dandelions are cool." "My daughter loves them."
"I once egged an old woman's house." I want
to suggest poetry itself depends on the pleasure
of phrases floating on air then taking root; instead
I tell them, "We don't have much time left," then
softly blow the question, "What do people think?"

On Finding Something To Say After a Reading

She stops me at the door to ask if I have any advice
for a young poet, and, for once, before I say something
flip or trite, I ask, "For you?" She nods, and I realize
she probably has been waiting all night to approach.
I try to think what might be useful, something beyond
the usual—"read," "write," "listen." If she isn't doing
these, telling her won't help. What about a koan?
Write what the river says to the trees. Write what
hasn't been written and must be. But I'm no monk.
I could shrug, insist, "No, I don't," but she's waited
too long now. Then I remember how before a game
my coach would say, "Run your ass off. Ignore
the scoreboard and bleachers. And damnit, have fun."
It reassured us then. Maybe it's enough for her now.

How to Write

Go to the bakery each morning.
Examine the muffins, bear claws,
croissants, danishes, and scones.
Consider the way they've been stacked,
their shapes and sizes, but do not buy
anything. Tell yourself that you might
get one later, as a reward for working,
although you know this is a lie. Take
your coffee to the sugar and creamers
and, as you go, note who is with
the retirees and who is missing today,
whether the pregnant cashier you saw
fighting with her boyfriend last week
is working, and which nurse has come
from the hospital across the street
to get the shift's bagels and coffees.
Browse your email, check the weather,
and read the *New York Times* headlines.
Listen to the people in the other booths
say things like "I know he's family now,
but I still hate that son-of-a-bitch," or
"What an interesting skill set you have.
Were you home-schooled?" Open a file,
type in parts of these conversations,
and assure yourself that recording
other people's words counts as writing.
Refill your coffee, log on to email again,

go to the bathroom, get out your daytimer
to see when you last had a check-up,
went to the dentist, or had the oil changed.
Open a file with an old piece of writing
and start to read. Become hopeful,
take notes, then decide, once again,
it's unfixable. Wonder why you bother.
There's no point really. So why not
eat something? Why not feel good
for a moment? Think about what kind
of muffin you won't buy yourself later,
maybe something with nuts, maybe
something with chocolate, or maybe
something you've never not had before,
something too fantastic to even imagine.

The Writing Teacher

He says take that
memory and make it
an essay.

He says try
turning that
essay into
a story.

He asks what if
the story
were changed
into a poem.

This is what
we have to do
he is saying

again and again

take this life,
turn it,
change it,
form it.

JOSEPH MILLS learned to drive on Indiana back roads. This is also where he learned about the importance of seat belts when he introduced his mother's Toyota Corolla to a telephone pole at 2 a.m. even though he had told her that he would only use the car to go to the laundrymat and grocery. His first car was a family hand-me-down, an Oldsmobile Vista Cruiser station wagon. It had a Rocket V8 engine, got eight miles to the gallon, and the one time he took it to a car wash he realized that he was spraying through the rusted door into the backseat. The first car he bought for himself was a Toyota pickup which he drove all over North America, getting it stuck on a Mexican beach during an incoming tide, in a Utah snowstorm, in a Florida marsh, and in traffic jams from New York to San Francisco. He cried when someone drove it out of his life. He now drives a mini-van.

LaVergne, TN USA
23 July 2010
190643LV00003B/41/P